Noah's Ark

A biblical and scientific look at the the Genesis account

P9-DMU-501

WAS THERE REALLY A NOAH'S ARK & FLOOD? • FLOOD LEGENDS • HAS NOAH'S ARK BEEN FOUND? • WHAT DID NOAH'S ARK LOOK LIKE? • CARING FOR THE ANIMALS ON THE ARK • HOW DID THE ANIMALS SPREAD ALL OVER THE WORLD? • THE ARK & THE GOSPEL

A POCKET GUIDE TO . . .

Noah's Ark

A biblical and scientific look at the the Genesis account

answersingenesis
Petersburg, Kentucky, USA

Seventh printing: February 2012

ISBN: 1-60092-252-X

Printed in China
www.answersingenesis.org

Table of Contents

Introduction

The idea of a man building a giant boat to rescue humanity has been the subject of much interest throughout human history. From Ark-themed bathrooms and nursery accessories to irreverent portrayals in modern films, Noah and his Ark have been represented in many different ways. The Ark is a common target for those who wish to mock the Bible or turn its historical accounts into fables with an element of moral teaching. Rather than taking the account in the Bible at face value, many allow a modern "scientific" mind-set to impact their understanding of Scripture.

But what did the Ark really look like? Does the Bible shed any light on the size or construction of the Ark? How does the Ark compare to the ships we have today? How did Noah round up all of the animals on the earth? Has Noah's Ark been found? Is there any symbolism in the Ark? All of these questions, and more, will be answered as you explore this book.

When you look to Scripture as the authoritative writing that it is, you would expect what you see in the world around you to confirm those truths. An understanding of the size and proportions of the Ark, and the biblical classification of the created kinds, are supported by what we observe in nature. When we look at the evidence through the lens of Scripture, what we see in the world supports the factual nature of the account of Noah and the Ark as recorded.

Was There Really a Noah's Ark?

by Ken Ham and Tim Lovett

*T*he account of Noah and the Ark is one of the most widely known events in the history of mankind. Unfortunately, like other Bible accounts, it is often taken as a mere fairy tale.

The Bible, though, is the true history book of the universe, and in that light, the most-asked questions about the Ark and Flood of Noah can be answered with authority and confidence.

How large was Noah's Ark?

"The length of the ark shall be three hundred cubits, its width fifty cubits, and its height thirty cubits" (Genesis 6:15).

Unlike many whimsical drawings that depict the Ark as some kind of overgrown houseboat (with giraffes sticking out the top), the Ark described in the Bible was a huge vessel. Not until the late 1800s was a ship built that exceeded the capacity of Noah's Ark.

Santa Maria Wyoming   Titanic   Queen Mary II

WOOD SHIPS   STEEL SHIPS

0   100 ft. 200 ft. 300 ft. 400 ft. 500 ft. 600 ft. 700 ft. 800 ft. 900 ft. 1000 ft. 1100 ft. 1200 ft.

Noah's Ark

The dimensions of the Ark are convincing for two reasons: the proportions are like that of a modern cargo ship, and it is about as large as a wooden ship can be built. The cubit gives us a good indication of size.[1] With the cubit's measurement, we know that the Ark must have been at least 450 feet (137 m) long, 75 feet (23 m) wide, and 45 feet (14 m) high. In the Western world, wooden sailing ships never got much longer than about 330 feet (100 m), yet the ancient Greeks built vessels at least this size 2,000 years earlier. China built huge wooden ships in the 1400s that may have been as large as the Ark. The biblical Ark is one of the largest wooden ships of all time—a mid-sized cargo ship by today's standards.

How could Noah build the Ark?

The Bible does not tell us that Noah and his sons built the Ark by themselves. Noah could have hired skilled laborers or had relatives, such as Methuselah and Lamech, help build the vessel. However, nothing indicates that they could not—or that they did not—build the Ark themselves in the time allotted. The physical strength and mental processes of men in Noah's day was at least as great as (quite likely, even superior to) our own.[2] They certainly would have had efficient means for harvesting and cutting timber, as well as for shaping, transporting, and erecting the massive beams and boards required.

If one or two men today can erect a large house in just 12 weeks, how much more could three or four men do in a few years? Adam's descendants were making complex musical instruments, forging metal, and building cities—their tools, machines, and techniques were not primitive.

History has shown that technology can be lost. In Egypt, China, and the Americas the earlier dynasties built more impressive buildings or had finer art or better science. Many so-called modern inventions turn out to be re-inventions, like concrete, which was used by the Romans.

Even accounting for the possible loss of technology due to the Flood, early post-Flood civilizations display all the engineering know-how necessary for a project like Noah's Ark. People sawing and drilling wood in Noah's day, only a few centuries before the Egyptians were sawing and drilling granite, is very reasonable! The idea that more primitive civilizations are further back in time is an evolutionary concept.

In reality, when God created Adam, he was perfect. Today, the individual human intellect has suffered from 6,000 years of sin and decay. The sudden rise in technology in the last few centuries has nothing to do with increasing intelligence; it is a combination of publishing and sharing ideas, and the spread of key inventions that became tools for investigation and manufacturing. One of the most recent tools is the computer, which compensates a great deal for our natural decline in mental performance and discipline, since it permits us to gather and store information as perhaps never before.

How could Noah round up so many animals?

Of the birds after their kind, of animals after their kind, and of every creeping thing of the earth after its kind, two of every kind will come to you, to keep them alive (Genesis 6:20).

This verse tells us that Noah didn't have to search or travel to far away places to bring the animals on board. The world map was completely different before the Flood, and on the basis of Genesis 1, there may have been only one continent. The animals simply arrived at the Ark as if called by a "homing instinct" (a behavior implanted in the animals by their Creator) and marched up the ramp, all by themselves.

Though this was probably a supernatural event (one that cannot be explained by our understanding of nature), compare it to the impressive migratory behavior we see in some animals today. We are still far from understanding all the marvelous animal behaviors exhibited in God's creation: the migration of

Canada geese and other birds, the amazing flights of Monarch butterflies, the annual travels of whales and fish, hibernation instincts, earthquake sensitivity, and countless other fascinating capabilities of God's animal kingdom.

Were dinosaurs on Noah's Ark?

The history of God's creation (told in Genesis 1 and 2) tells us that all the land-dwelling creatures were made on Day 6 of Creation Week—the same day God made Adam and Eve. Therefore, it is clear that dinosaurs (being land animals) were made with man.

Also, two of every kind (seven of some) of land animal boarded the Ark. Nothing indicates that any of the land animal kinds were already extinct before the Flood. Besides, the description of "behemoth" in chapter 40 of the book of Job (Job lived after the Flood) only fits with something like a sauropod dinosaur. The ancestor of "behemoth" must have been on board the Ark.[3]

We also find many dinosaurs that were trapped and fossilized in Flood sediment. Widespread legends of encounters with dragons give another indication that at least some dinosaurs survived the Flood. The only way this could happen is if they were on the Ark.

Juveniles of even the largest land animals do not present a size problem, and, being young, they

AFTER EDEN by Dan Lietha

HOW COULD NOAH HAVE POSSIBLY FIT **DINOSAURS** IN THE ARK?

HOW WAS IT POSSIBLE FOR YOUR MOTHER TO GIVE BIRTH TO **YOU**?

www.AnswersInGenesis.org

© 2001 AiG

Even the largest full-grown creatures were once small!

have their full breeding life ahead of them. Yet most dinosaurs were not very large at all—some were the size of a chicken (although absolutely no relation to birds, as many evolutionists are now saying). Most scientists agree that the average size of a dinosaur is actually the size of a sheep.

For example, God most likely brought Noah two young adult sauropods (e.g., apatosaurs), rather than two full-grown sauropods. The same goes for elephants, giraffes, and other animals that grow to be very large. However, there was adequate room for most fully grown adult animals anyway.

As far as the number of different types of dinosaurs, it should be recognized that, although there are hundreds of names for different varieties (species) of dinosaurs that have been discovered, there are probably only about 50 actual different kinds.

How could Noah fit all the animals on the Ark?

And of every living thing of all flesh you shall bring two of every sort into the ark, to keep them alive with you; they shall be male and female (Genesis 6:19).

In the book *Noah's Ark: A Feasibility Study*,[4] creationist researcher John Woodmorappe suggests that, at most, 16,000 animals were all that were needed to preserve the created kinds that God brought into the Ark.

The Ark did not need to carry every kind of animal—nor did God command it. It carried only air-breathing, land-dwelling animals, creeping things, and winged animals such as birds. Aquatic life (fish, whales, etc.) and many amphibious creatures could have survived in sufficient numbers outside the Ark. This cuts down significantly the total number of animals that needed to be on board.

Another factor which greatly reduces the space requirements is the fact that the tremendous variety in species we see today did not exist in the days of Noah. Only the parent "kinds" of these species were required to be on board in order to repopulate the earth.[5] For example, only two dogs were needed to give rise to all the dog species that exist today.

Creationist estimates for the maximum number of animals that would have been necessary to come on board the Ark have ranged from a few thousand to 35,000, but they may be as few as two thousand if the biblical kind is approximately the same as the modern family classification.

As stated before, Noah wouldn't have taken the largest animals onto the Ark; it is more likely he took juveniles aboard the Ark to repopulate the earth after the Flood was over. These younger animals also require less space, less food, and have less waste.

Using a short cubit of 18 inches (46 cm) for the Ark to be conservative, Woodmorappe's conclusion is that "less than half of the cumulative area of the Ark's three decks need to have been occupied by the animals and their enclosures."[6] This meant there was plenty of room for fresh food, water, and even many other people.

How did Noah care for all the animals?

Just as God brought the animals to Noah by some form of supernatural means, He surely also prepared them for this amazing event. Creation scientists suggest that God gave the animals the ability to hibernate, as we see in many species today. Most animals react to natural disasters in ways that were designed to help them survive. It's very possible many animals did hibernate, perhaps even supernaturally intensified by God.

Whether it was supernatural or simply a normal response to the darkness and confinement of a rocking ship, the fact that God told Noah to build rooms (*qen*—literally in Hebrew "nests") in Genesis 6:14 implies that the animals were subdued or nesting. God also told Noah to take food for them (Genesis 6:21), which tells us that they were not in a year-long coma either.

Were we able to walk through the Ark as it was being built, we would undoubtedly be amazed at the ingenious systems on board for water and food storage and distribution. As Woodmorappe explains in *Noah's Ark: A Feasibility Study*, a small group of farmers today can raise thousands of cattle and other animals in a very small space. One can easily imagine all kinds of devices on the Ark that would have enabled a small number of people to feed and care for the animals, from watering to waste removal.

As Woodmorappe points out, no special devices were needed for eight people to care for 16,000 animals. But if they existed, how would these devices be powered? There are all sorts of possibilities. How about a plumbing system for gravity-fed drinking water, a ventilation system driven by wind or wave motion, or hoppers that dispense grain as the animals eat it? None of these require higher technology than what we know existed in ancient cultures. And yet these cultures were likely well-short of the skill and capability of Noah and the pre-Flood world. (For more on how Noah may have cared for the animals on the Ark, see chapter 4, "Caring for the Animals on the Ark.")

How could a flood destroy every living thing?

And all flesh died that moved on the earth: birds and cattle and beasts and every creeping thing that creeps on the earth, and every man. All in whose nostrils was the breath of the spirit of life, all that was on the dry land, died (Genesis 7:21–22).

Noah's Flood was much more destructive than any 40-day rainstorm ever could be. Scripture says that the "fountains of the great deep" broke open. In other words, earthquakes, volcanoes, and geysers of molten lava and scalding water were squeezed out of the earth's crust in a violent, explosive upheaval. These fountains were not stopped until 150 days into the Flood—so the earth was literally churning underneath the waters for about five months!

The duration of the Flood was extensive, and Noah and his family were aboard the Ark for over a year.

Relatively recent local floods, volcanoes, and earthquakes—though clearly devastating to life and land—are tiny in comparison to the worldwide catastrophe that destroyed "the world that then existed" (2 Peter 3:6). All land animals and people not on board the Ark were destroyed in the floodwaters—billions of animals were preserved in the great fossil record we see today.

How could the Ark survive the Flood?

The description of the Ark is very brief—Genesis 6:14–16. Those three verses contain critical information including overall dimensions, but Noah was almost certainly given more detail than this. Other divinely specified constructions in the Bible are meticulously detailed, like the descriptions of Moses's Tabernacle or the temple in Ezekiel's vision.

The Bible does not say the Ark was a rectangular box. In fact, Scripture gives no clue about the shape of Noah's Ark other than the proportions—length, width, and depth. Ships have long been described like this without ever implying a block-shaped hull.

Moses used the obscure term *tebah*, a word that is only used again for the basket that carried baby Moses (Exodus 2:3). One was a huge wooden ship and the other a tiny wicker basket. Both float, both rescue life, and both are covered. But the similarity ends there. We can be quite sure that the baby basket did not have the same proportions as the Ark, and Egyptian baskets of the time were typically rounded. Perhaps *tebah* means "lifeboat."

For many years biblical creationists have simply depicted the Ark as a rectangular box. This shape helped illustrate its size while avoiding the distractions of hull curvature. It also made it easy to compare volume. By using a short cubit and the maximum number of animal "kinds," creationists, as we've seen, have demonstrated how easily the Ark could fit the payload.[7] At the time, space was the main issue; other factors were secondary.

However, the next phase of research investigated sea-keeping (behavior and comfort at sea), hull strength, and stability. This began with a Korean study performed at the world-class ship research center (KRISO) in 1992.[8] The team of nine KRISO researchers was led by Dr. Hong, who is now director-general of the research center.

The study confirmed that the Ark could handle waves as high as 98 feet (30 m), and that the proportions of the biblical Ark are near optimal—an interesting admission from Dr. Hong, who believes evolutionary ideas, openly claiming "life came from the sea."[9] The study combined analysis, model wave testing, and ship standards, yet the concept was simple: compare the biblical Ark with 12 other vessels of the same volume but modified in length, width, or depth. Three qualities were measured—stability, hull strength, and comfort.

Ship qualities measured in the 1992 Korean study

While Noah's Ark was an average performer in each quality, it was among the best designs overall. In other words, the proportions show a careful design balance that is easily lost when proportions are modified the wrong way. It is no surprise that modern ships have similar proportions—those proportions work.

Interesting to note is the fact that this study makes nonsense of the claim that Genesis was written only a few centuries before Christ and was based on flood legends such as the Epic of Gilgamesh. The Babylonian ark is a cube shape, something so far from reality that even the shortest hull in the Korean study was not even close. But we would expect mistakes from other flood accounts, like that of Gilgamesh, as the account of Noah would have been distorted as it was passed down through different cultures.

Yet one mystery remained. The Korean study did not hide the fact that some shorter hulls slightly outperformed the biblical Noah's Ark. Further work by Tim Lovett, one author of this chapter, and two naval architects, Jim King and Dr. Allen Magnuson, focused attention on the issue of broaching— being turned sideways by the waves.

How do we know what the waves were like? If there were no waves at all, stability, comfort, or strength would be unimportant, and the proportions would not matter. A shorter hull would then be a more efficient volume, taking less wood and less work. However, we can take clues from the proportions of the Ark itself. The Korean study had assumed waves came from every direction, giving shorter hulls an advantage. But real ocean waves usually have a dominant direction due to the wind, favoring a short, wide hull even more.

Another type of wave may also have affected the Ark during the Flood—tsunamis. Earthquakes can create tsunamis that devastate coastlines. However, when a tsunami travels in deep water it is imperceptible to a ship. During the Flood, the water would have been very deep—there is enough water in today's oceans to cover the earth to a depth of about 1.7 miles (2.7 km). The Bible states that the Ark rose "high above the earth" (Genesis 7:17). Launched from high ground by the rising floodwaters, the Ark would have avoided the initial devastation of coastlines and low-lying areas, and remained safe from tsunamis throughout the voyage.

After several months at sea, God sent a wind (Genesis 8:1), which could have produced very large waves since these waves can be produced by a strong, steady wind. Open-water testing confirms that any drifting vessel will naturally turn side-on to the waves (broach). With waves approaching the side of the vessel (beam sea), a long vessel like the Ark would be trapped in an uncomfortable situation; in heavy weather it could become dangerous. This could be overcome, however, by the ves-

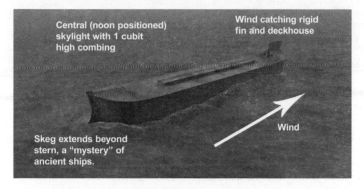

Central (noon positioned) skylight with 1 cubit high combing

Wind catching rigid fin and deckhouse

Skeg extends beyond stern, a "mystery" of ancient ships.

Wind

sel catching the wind (Genesis 8:1) at the bow and catching the water at the stern—aligning itself like a wind vane. These features appear to have inspired a number of ancient ship designs. Once the Ark points into the waves, the long, ship-like proportions create a more comfortable and controlled voyage. Traveling slowly with the wind, it had no need for speed, but the Bible does say the Ark moved about on the surface of the waters (Genesis 7:18).

Compared to a ship-like bow and stern, blunt ends are not as strong, have edges that are vulnerable to damage during launch and beaching, and give a rougher ride. Since the Bible gives proportions like that of a true ship, it makes sense that it should look and act ship-like. The design below is an attempt to flesh out the biblical outline using real-life experiments and archeological evidence of ancient ships.

While Scripture does not point out a wind-catching feature at the bow, the abbreviated account we are given in Genesis makes no mention of drinking water, the number of animals, or the way they got out of the Ark either.

Nothing in this newly depicted Ark contradicts Scripture; in fact, it shows how accurate Scripture is! (For more information on the design of the Ark, see chapter 3, "Thinking Outside the Box.")

Where did all the water go?

And the waters receded continually from the earth. At the end of the hundred and fifty days the waters decreased (Genesis 8:3).

Simply put, the water from the Flood is in the oceans and seas we see today. Three-quarters of the earth's surface is covered with water.

As even secular geologists observe, it does appear that the continents were at one time "together" and not separated by the vast oceans of today. The forces involved in the Flood were certainly sufficient to change all of this.

Scripture indicates that God formed the ocean basins, raising the land out of the water, so that the floodwaters returned to a safe place. (Some theologians believe Psalm 104 may refer to this event.) Some creation scientists believe this breakup of the continent was part of the mechanism that ultimately caused the Flood.[11]

Some have speculated, because of Genesis 10:25, that the continental break occurred during the time of Peleg. However, this division is mentioned in the context of the Tower of Babel's language division of the whole earth (Genesis 10–11). So the context points to a dividing of the languages and people groups, not the land breaking apart.

If there were a massive movement of continents during the time of Peleg, there would have been another worldwide flood. The Bible indicates that the mountains of Ararat existed for the Ark to land in them (Genesis 8:4); so the Indian-Australian Plate and Eurasian Plate had to have already collided, indicating that the continents had already shifted prior to Peleg.

Was Noah's Flood global?

And the waters prevailed exceedingly on the earth, and all the high hills under the whole heaven were covered. The waters prevailed fifteen cubits upward, and the mountains were covered (Genesis 7:19–20).

Many Christians today claim that the Flood of Noah's time was only a local flood. These people generally believe in a local flood because they have accepted the widely believed evolutionary history of the earth, which interprets fossil layers as the history of the sequential appearance of life over millions of years.[12]

Scientists once understood the fossils, which are buried in water-carried sediments of mud and sand, to be mostly the result of the great Flood. Those who now accept millions of years of gradual accumulation of fossils have, in their way of thinking, explained away the evidence for the global Flood. Hence, many compromising Christians insist on a local flood.

Secularists deny the possibility of a worldwide Flood at all. If they would think from a biblical perspective, however, they would see the abundant evidence for the global Flood. As someone once quipped, "I wouldn't have seen it if I hadn't believed it."

A local flood that rose above the mountains?

Those who accept the evolutionary time frame, with its fossil accumulation, also rob the Fall of Adam of its serious consequences. They put the fossils, which testify of disease, suffering, and death, before Adam and Eve sinned and brought death and suffering into the world. In doing this, they also undermine the meaning of the death and resurrection of Christ. Such a scenario also robs all meaning from God's description of His finished creation as "very good."

If the Flood only affected the area of Mesopotamia, as some claim, why did Noah have to build an Ark? He could have walked to the other side of the mountains and escaped. Most importantly, if the Flood were local, people not living in the vicinity of the Flood would not have been affected by it. They would have escaped God's judgment on sin.

In addition, Jesus believed that the Flood killed every person not on the Ark. What else could Christ mean when He likened the coming world judgment to the judgment of "all" men in the days of Noah (Matthew 24:37–39)?

In 2 Peter 3, the coming judgment by fire is likened to the former judgment by water in Noah's Flood. A partial judgment in Noah's day, therefore, would mean a partial judgment to come.

If the Flood were only local, how could the waters rise to 20 feet (6 m) above the mountains (Genesis 7:20)? Water seeks its own level; it could not rise to cover the local mountains while leaving the rest of the world untouched.

Even what is now Mt. Everest was once covered with water and uplifted afterward.[13] If we even out the ocean basins and flatten out the mountains, there is enough water to cover the entire earth by about 1.7 miles (2.7 km).[14] Also important to note is that, with the leveling out of the oceans and mountains, the Ark would not have been riding at the height of the current Mt. Everest, thus no need for such things as oxygen masks either.

There's more. If the Flood were a local flood, God would have repeatedly broken His promise never to send such a flood again. God put a rainbow in the sky as a covenant between God and man and the animals that He would never repeat such an event. There have been huge local floods in recent times (e.g., in Bangladesh); but never has there been another global Flood that killed all life on the land.

Where Is the evidence in the earth for Noah's Flood?

For this they willingly forget: that by the word of God the heavens were of old, and the earth standing out of water and in the water, by which the world that then existed perished, being flooded with water (2 Peter 3:5–6).

Evidence of Noah's Flood can be seen all over the earth, from seabeds to mountaintops. Whether you travel by car, train, or plane, the physical features of the earth's terrain clearly indicate a catastrophic past, from canyons and craters to coal beds and caverns. Some layers of strata extend across continents, revealing the effects of a huge catastrophe. You can read more about the Flood and the geological evidence in the earth in our *Pocket Guide to the Flood*.

The earth's crust has massive amounts of layered sedimentary rock, sometimes miles (kilometers) deep! These layers of sand, soil, and material—mostly laid down by water—were once soft like mud, but they are now hard stone. Encased in these sedimentary layers are billions of dead things (fossils of plants and animals) buried very quickly. The evidence all over the earth is staring everyone in the face.

Where is Noah's Ark today?

Then the Ark rested in the seventh month, the seventeenth day of the month, on the mountains of Ararat (Genesis 8:4).

The Ark landed in mountains. The ancient name for these mountains could refer to several areas in the Middle East, such as Mt. Ararat in Turkey or other mountain ranges in neighboring countries.

Mt. Ararat has attracted the most attention because it has permanent ice, and some people report having seen the Ark. Many expeditions have searched for the Ark there. There is no conclusive evidence of the Ark's location or survival; after all, it landed on the mountains about 4,500 years ago. Also it could easily have deteriorated, been destroyed, or been used as lumber by Noah and his descendants.

Some scientists and Bible scholars, though, believe the Ark could indeed be preserved—perhaps to be providentially revealed at a future time as a reminder of the past judgment and the judgment to come, although the same could be said for things like the Ark of the Covenant or other biblical icons. Jesus said, "If they do not hear Moses and the prophets, neither will they be persuaded though one rise from the dead" (Luke 16:31).

The Ark is unlikely to have survived without supernatural intervention, but this is neither promised nor expected from Scripture. However, it is a good idea to check if it still exists. (For more information on the search for Noah's Ark, see chapter 5, "Has Noah's Ark Been Found?").

Why did God destroy the earth that He had made?

Then the Lord saw that the wickedness of man was great in the earth, and that every intent of the thoughts of his heart was only evil continually. But Noah found grace in the eyes of the Lord (Genesis 6:5, 8).

These verses speak for themselves. Every human being on the face of the earth had turned after the wickedness in their own hearts, but Noah, because of his righteousness before God, was spared from God's judgment, along with his wife, their sons, and their wives. As a result of man's wickedness, God sent judgment on all mankind. As harsh as the destruction was, no living person was without excuse.

God also used the Flood to separate and to purify those who believed in Him from those who didn't. Throughout history and throughout the Bible, this cycle has taken place time after time: separation, purification, judgment, and redemption.

Without God and without a true knowledge and understanding of Scripture, which provides the true history of the world, man is doomed to repeat the same mistakes over and over again.

How is Christ like the Ark?

For the Son of Man has come to save that which was lost (Matthew 18:11).

As God's Son, the Lord Jesus Christ is like Noah's Ark. Jesus came to seek and to save the lost. Just as Noah and his family were saved by the Ark, rescued by God from the floodwaters, so anyone who believes in Jesus as Lord and Savior will be spared from the coming final judgment of mankind, rescued by God from the fire that will destroy the earth after the last days (2 Peter 3:7).

Noah and his family had to go through a doorway into the Ark to be saved, and the Lord shut the door behind them (Genesis 7:16). So we too have to go through a "doorway" to be saved so that we won't be eternally separated from God. The Son of God, Jesus, stepped into history to pay the penalty for our sin of rebellion. Jesus said, "I am the door. If anyone enters by Me, he will be saved, and will go in and out and find pasture" (John 10:9).

---

1. The cubit was defined as the length of the forearm from elbow to fingertip. Ancient cubits vary anywhere from 17.5 inches (45 cm) to 22 inches (56 cm), the longer sizes dominating the major ancient constructions. Despite this, even a conservative 18 inch (46 cm) cubit describes a sizeable vessel.

2. For the evidence, see Donald Chittick, *The Puzzle of Ancient Man* (Newberg, OR: Creation

---

Compass, 1998). This book details evidence of man's intelligence in early post-Flood civilizations.

3. For some remarkable evidence that dinosaurs have lived until relatively recent times, see chapter 12 of *The New Answers Book 1* (Green Forest, AR: Master Books, 2006). Also read Ken Ham, *The Great Dinosaur Mystery Solved* (Green Forest, AR: Master Books, 2000). Also visit www.answersingenesis.org/go/dinosaurs.

4. John Woodmorappe, *Noah's Ark: A Feasibility Study* (Santee, CA: Institute for Creation Research, 2003).

5. Here's one example: more than 200 different breeds of dogs exist today, from the miniature poodle to the St. Bernard—all of which have descended from one original dog "kind" (as have the wolf, dingo, etc.). Many other types of animals—cat kind, horse kind, cow kind, etc.—have similarly been naturally and selectively bred to achieve the wonderful variation in species that we have today. God "programmed" this variety into the genetic code of all animal kinds—even humankind! God also made it impossible for the basic "kinds" of animals to breed and reproduce with each other. For example, cats and dogs cannot breed to make a new type of creature. This is by God's design, and it is one fact that makes evolution impossible.

6. John Woodmorappe, *Noah's Ark: A Feasibility Study*, p. 16.

7. Ibid.

8. Seok Won Hong et al., "Safety Investigation of Noah's Ark in a Seaway," *TJ* 8 no. 1 (1994): 26–36, www.answersingenesis.org/tj/v8/i1/noah.asp.

9. Seok Won Hong, "Warm greetings from the Director-General of MOERI (former KRISO), Director-General of MOERI/KORDI," http://www.moeri.re.kr/eng/about/about.htm.

10. For deeper study on this, please see Nozomi Osanai, "A Comparison of Scientific Reliability, A comparative study of the flood accounts in the Gilgamesh Epic and Genesis," Answers in Genesis, http://www.answersingenesis.org/go/gilgamesh.

11. See chapter 14 of *The New Answers Book 1* (Green Forest, AR: Master Books, 2006).

12. For compelling evidence that the earth is not billions of years old, read *The Young Earth* by Dr. John Morris and *Thousands . . . not Billions* by Dr. Don DeYoung; also see www.answersingenesis.org/go/young.

13. Mount Everest is more than 5 miles (8 km) high. How, then, could the Flood have covered "all the mountains under the whole heaven?" Before the Flood, the mountains were not so high. The mountains today were formed only towards the end of, and after, the Flood by collision of the tectonic plates and the associated up-thrusting. In support of this, the layers that form the uppermost parts of Mt. Everest are themselves composed of fossil-bearing, water-deposited layers.

14. A.R. Wallace, *Man's Place in the Universe* (New York: McClure, Phillips & Co, 1903), pp. 225–226; www.wku.edu/~smithch/wallace/S728-3.htm.

Ken Ham is President and CEO of Answers in Genesis–USA and the Creation Museum. Ken's bachelor's degree in applied science (with an emphasis on environmental biology) was awarded by the Queensland Institute of Technology in Australia. He also holds a diploma of education from the University of Queensland. In recognition of the contribution Ken has made to the church in the USA and internationally, Ken has been awarded two honorary doctorates: a Doctor of Divinity (1997) from Temple Baptist College in Cincinnati, Ohio and a Doctor of Literature (2004) from Liberty University in Lynchburg, Virginia.

Ken has authored or co-authored many books concerning the authority and accuracy of God's Word and the effects of evolutionary thinking, including *Genesis of a Legacy* and *The Lie: Evolution*.

Since moving to America in 1987, Ken has become one of the most in-demand Christian conference speakers and talk show guests in America. He has appeared on national shows such as Fox's *The O'Reilly Factor* and *Fox and Friends in the Morning*; CNN's *The Situation Room with Wolf Blitzer*, ABC's *Good Morning America*, the BBC, *CBS News Sunday Morning*, *The NBC Nightly News with Brian Williams*, and *The PBS News Hour with Jim Lehrer*.

Tim Lovett earned his degree in mechanical engineering from Sydney University (Australia) and was an instructor for 12 years in technical college engineering courses. Tim has studied the Flood and the Ark for 13 years and is widely recognized for his cutting-edge research on the design and structure of Noah's Ark.

Flood Legends: A World of Stories Based on Truth

by A. J. Monty White

There are hundreds of stories and legends about a worldwide flood. Why do diverse cultures share a strikingly similar story?

Did you know that stories about a worldwide flood are found in historic records all over the world? According to Dr. Duane Gish in his popular book *Dinosaurs by Design*, there are more than 270 such stories, most of which share a common theme and similar characters. So many flood stories with such similarities surely come from the Flood of Noah's day.

A historical event

The worldwide catastrophic Flood, recorded in the book of Genesis, was a real event that affected real people. In fact, those people carried the knowledge of this event with them when they spread to the ends of the earth.

The Bible declares that the earth-covering cataclysm of Noah's day is an obvious fact of history. People "willfully forget: that . . . the world that then existed perished, being flooded with water" (2 Peter 3:5–6). This Flood left many evidences, from the fact that over 70% of the rocks on continents were laid down by water and contain fossils, to the widespread flood legends. Both of these evidences provide compelling support for this historical event.

If only eight people—Noah's family—survived the Flood, we would expect there to be historical evidence of a worldwide flood. If you think about it, the evidence would be historical records in the nations of the world, and this is what we have, as the chart [at right] indicates. Stories of the Flood—distorted though they may be—exist in practically all nations, from ancient Babylon onward. This evidence must not be lightly dismissed. If there never was a worldwide Flood, then why are there so many stories about it?

From generation to generation

The reason for these flood stories is not difficult to understand. When we turn to the history book of the universe, the Bible, we learn that Noah's descendants stayed together for approximately 100 years, until God confused their languages at Babel (Genesis 11:1–9). As these people moved away from Babel, their descendants formed nations based primarily on the languages they shared in common. Through those languages, the story of the Flood was shared, until it became embedded in their cultural history.

Similar stories

Hawaiians have a flood story that tells of a time when, long after the death of the first man, the world became a wicked, terrible place. Only one good man was left, and his name was Nu-u. He made a great canoe with a house on it and filled it with animals. In this story, the waters came up over all the earth and killed all the people; only Nu-u and his family were saved.

Another flood story is from China. It records that Fuhi, his wife, three sons, and three daughters escaped a great flood and were the only people alive on earth. After the great flood, they repopulated the world.

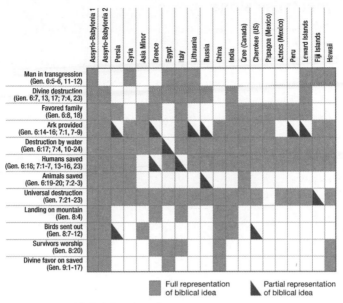

	Assyrio-Babylonia 1	Assyrio-Babylonia 2	Persia	Syria	Asia Minor	Greece	Egypt	Italy	Lithuania	Russia	China	India	Cree (Canada)	Cherokee (US)	Papagoa (Mexico)	Aztecs (Mexico)	Peru	Leward Islands	Fiji Islands	Hawaii

Full representation of biblical idea   **Partial representation of biblical idea**

Rows:
Man in transgression (Gen. 6:5-6, 11-12)
Divine destruction (Gen. 6:7, 13, 17; 7:4, 23)
Favored family (Gen. 6:8, 18)
Ark provided (Gen. 6:14-16; 7:1, 7-9)
Destruction by water (Gen. 6:17; 7:4, 10-24)
Humans saved (Gen. 6:18; 7:1-7, 13-16, 23)
Animals saved (Gen. 6:19-20; 7:2-3)
Universal destruction (Gen. 7:21-23)
Landing on mountain (Gen. 8:4)
Birds sent out (Gen. 8:7-12)
Survivors worship (Gen. 8:20)
Divine favor on saved (Gen. 9:1-17)

Global flood traditions

This chart shows the similarities that several myths have with the Genesis account of Noah's Flood. Although there are varying degrees of accuracy, these legends and stories all contain similarities to aspects of the same historical event—Noah's Flood.

Chart adapted from B.C. Nelson, *The Deluge Story in Stone*, Appendix 11: Flood Traditions, Figure 38 (Minneapolis, Minnesota: Augsburg, 1931).

As the story of the Flood was verbally passed from one generation to the next, some aspects would have been lost or altered. And this is what has happened, as we can see from the chart. However, as seen in the given examples, each story shares remarkable similarities to the account of Noah in the Bible. This is true even in some of the details, such as the name Nu-u in the Hawaiian flood story. "Nu-u" is very similar to "Noah."

What these stories mean

God clearly sent a worldwide Flood to punish humankind for their evil and corrupt ways (Genesis 6:5, 11). Even though Flood-affirming evidence from geology and other areas of study is abundant, we don't need this evidence to know what happened. Starting with the Bible and the history that God faithfully recorded there, Christians have a tool to interpret the evidence that evolutionists and non-Christians do not. We have the record of what happened, from the One who was there.

Monty White earned his BSc degree in chemistry and his PhD in gas kinetics from the University of Wales, Aberystwyth. Dr. White is the former CEO of Answers in Genesis-UK/Europe and has traveled extensively throughout Europe lecturing on creationists' views of origins.

Thinking Outside the Box

by Tim Lovett

While the Bible gives us essential details on many things, including the size and proportions of Noah's Ark, it does not necessarily specify the precise shape of this vessel. It is important to understand, however, that this lack of physical description is consistent with other historical accounts in Scripture.[1] So how should we illustrate what the Ark looked like? The two main options include a default rectangular shape reflecting the lack of specific detail, and a more fleshed-out design that incorporates principles of ship design from maritime science, while remaining consistent with the Bible's size and proportions.

Genesis describes the Ark in three verses, which require careful examination:

6:14—"Make yourself an ark [*tebah*] of gopher wood; make rooms [*qinniym*] in the ark, and cover it inside and outside with pitch [*kofer*].

6:15—"And this is how you shall make it: The length of the ark shall be three hundred cubits, its width fifty cubits, and its height thirty cubits.

6:16—"You shall make a window [*tsohar*] for the ark, and you shall finish it to a cubit from above; and set the door of the ark in its side. You shall make it with lower, second, and third decks."

Most Bibles make some unusual translation choices for certain key words. Elsewhere in the Bible the Hebrew word translated here as "rooms" is usually rendered "nests"; "pitch" would normally be called "covering"; and "window" would be "noon light." Using these more typical meanings, the Ark would be something like this:

The *tebah* (Ark) was made from gopher wood, it had nests inside, and it was covered with a pitch-like substance inside and out. It was 300 cubits long, 50 cubits wide, and 30 cubits high. It had a noon light that ended a cubit upward and above, it had a door in the side, and there were three decks.

As divine specifications go, Moses offered more elaborate details about the construction of the Tabernacle, which suggests this might be the abridged version of Noah's complete directions. On the other hand, consider how wise Noah must have been after having lived several centuries. The instructions that we have recorded in Genesis may be all he needed to be told. But in any case, 300 cubits is a big ship, not some whimsical houseboat with giraffe necks sticking out the top.

Scripture gives no clue about the shape of Noah's Ark beyond its proportions—length, breadth, and depth. Ships have long been described like this without ever implying a block-shaped hull.

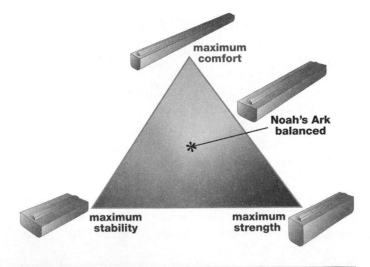

The scale of the Ark is huge yet remarkably realistic when compared to the largest wooden ships in history. The proportions are even more amazing—they are just like a modern cargo ship.

Scientific study endorses seaworthiness of Ark

Noah's Ark was the focus of a major 1992 scientific study headed by Dr. Seon Hong at the world-class ship research center KRISO, based in Daejeon, South Korea. Dr. Hong's team compared twelve hulls of different proportions to discover which design was most practical. No hull shape was found to significantly outperform the 4,300-year-old biblical design. In fact, the Ark's careful balance is easily lost if the proportions are modified, rendering the vessel either unstable, prone to fracture, or dangerously uncomfortable.

The research team found that the proportions of Noah's Ark carefully balanced the conflicting demands of stability (resistance to capsizing), comfort (seakeeping), and strength. In fact, the Ark has the same proportions as a modern cargo ship.

The study also confirmed that the Ark could handle waves as high as 100 feet (30 m). Dr. Hong is now director general of the facility and claims "life came from the sea," clearly not the words of a creationist on a mission to promote the worldwide Flood. Endorsing the seaworthiness of Noah's Ark obviously did not damage Dr. Hong's credibility.

Dr. Seon Won Hong was principal research scientist when he headed up the Noah's Ark investigation. In May 2005 Dr. Hong was appointed director general of MOERI (formerly KRISO). Dr. Hong earned a BS degree in naval architecture from Seoul National University and a PhD degree in applied mechanics from the University of Michigan, Ann Arbor.

All this makes nonsense of the claim that Genesis was written only a few centuries before Christ, as a mere retelling of earlier Babylonian flood legends such as the *Epic of Gilgamesh*. The *Epic of Gilgamesh* story describes a cube-shaped ark, which would have given a dangerously rough ride. This is neither accurate nor scientific. Noah's Ark is the original, while the Gilgamesh Epic is a later distortion.

What about the shape?

For many years biblical creationists have simply depicted the Ark as a rectangular box. This helped emphasize its size. It was easy to explain capacity and illustrate how easily the Ark could have handled the payload. With the rectangular shape, the Ark's stability against rolling could even be demonstrated by simple calculations.

Yet the Bible does not say the Ark must be a rectangular box. In fact, Scripture does not elaborate about the shape of Noah's Ark beyond those superb, overall proportions—length, breadth, and depth. Ships have long been described like this without implying a block-shaped hull.

In Hebrew "Ark" is the obscure term *tebah*, a word that appears only one other time when it describes the basket that carried baby Moses (Exodus 2:3). One was a huge, wooden ship and the other a tiny, wicker basket. Both floated, both preserved life, and both were covered; but the similarity ends there. If the word implied anything about shape, it would be "an Egyptian basket-like shape," typically rounded. More likely, however, *tebah* means something else, like "lifeboat."[2]

The Bible leaves the details regarding the shape of the Ark wide open—anything from a rectangular box with hard right angles and no curvature at all, to a ship-like form. Box-like has the largest carrying capacity, but a ship-like design would be safer and more comfortable in heavy seas. Such discussion is irrelevant if God intended to sustain the Ark no matter how well designed and executed.

Clues from the Bible

Some question whether the Ark was actually built to handle rough seas, but the Bible gives some clues about the sea conditions during the Flood:

- The Ark had the proportions of a seagoing vessel built for waves (Genesis 6:15).

- Logically, a mountain-covering, global Flood would not be dead calm (Genesis 7:19).

- The Ark moved about on the surface of the waters (Genesis 7:18).

- God made a wind to pass over the earth (Genesis 8:1).
- The Hebrew word for the Flood (*mabbul*) could imply being carried along.

The 1993 Korean study showed that some shorter hulls slightly outperformed the Ark model with biblical proportions. The study assumed waves came from every direction, favoring shorter hulls like that of a modern lifeboat. So why was Noah's Ark so long if it didn't need to be streamlined for moving through the water?

The answer lies in ride comfort (seakeeping). This requires a longer hull, at the cost of strength and stability, not to mention more wood. The Ark's high priority for comfort suggests that the anticipated waves must have been substantial.

Designed for tsunamis

Was the Ark designed for tsunamis? Not really. Tsunamis devastate coastlines, but when a tsunami travels in deep water, it is almost imperceptible to a ship. During the Flood, the water was probably very deep—there is enough water in today's oceans to cover a relatively flat earth to a consistent depth of over 2 miles (3.2 km). The Bible states that the Ark rose "high above the earth" (Genesis 7:17) and was stranded early (Genesis 8:4), before mountaintops were seen. If the launch was a mirror of the landing—the Ark being the last thing to float—it would have been a deep-water voyage from start to finish.

The worst waves may have been caused by wind, just like today. After several months at sea, God made a wind to pass over the earth. This suggests a large-scale weather pattern likely to produce waves with a dominant direction. It is an established fact that such waves would cause any drifting vessel to be driven sideways (broaching). A long vessel like the Ark would remain locked in this sideways position, an uncomfortable and even dangerous situation in heavy weather.

However, broaching can be avoided if the vessel catches the wind at one end and is "rooted" in the water at the other—turning like a weather vane into the wind. Once the Ark points into the waves, the long proportions create a more comfortable and controlled voyage. It had no need for speed, but the Ark did "move about on the surface of the waters."

The box-like Ark is not entirely disqualified as a safe option, but sharp edges are more vulnerable to damage during launch and landing. Blunt ends would also produce a rougher ride and allow the vessel to be more easily thrown around (but, of course, God could have miraculously kept the ship's precious cargo safe, regardless of the comfort factor). Since the Bible gives proportions consistent with those of a true cargo ship, it makes sense that it should look and act like a ship, too.

Coincidentally, certain aspects of this design appear in some of the earliest large ships depicted in pottery from Mesopotamia, which is not long after the Flood. It makes sense that shipwrights, who are conservative as a rule, would continue to include elements of the only ship to survive the global Flood—Noah's Ark.

Scripture does not record direction-keeping features attached to the Ark. They might have been obvious to a 500-year-old, or perhaps they were common among ships in Noah's day as they were afterwards. At the same time, the brief specifications in Genesis make no mention of other important details, such as storage of drinking water, disposal of excrement, or the way to get out of the Ark. Obviously Noah needed to know how many animals were coming, but this is not recorded either.

The Bible gives clear instruction for the construction of a number of things, but it does not specify many aspects of the Ark's construction. Nothing in this newly depicted Ark contradicts Scripture, even though it may be different from more accepted designs. But this design, in fact, shows us just how reasonable Scripture is as it depicts a stable, comfortable, and seaworthy vessel that was capable of fulfilling all the requirements stated in Scripture.

Details of design

Scripture gives no clue about the details of Noah's Ark beyond its proportions that are given in Genesis 6:15, which reads: "And this is how you shall make it: The length of the ark shall be three hundred cubits, its width fifty cubits, and its height thirty cubits." This new design incorporates the following features that are found on ancient ocean-going vessels.

1. Something to catch the wind

Wind-driven waves would cause a drifting vessel to turn dangerously side-on to the weather. However, such waves could be safely navigated by making the Ark steer itself with a wind-

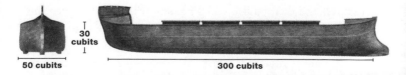

50 cubits

30 cubits

300 cubits

catching obstruction on the bow. To be effective, this obstruction must be large enough to overcome the turning effect of the waves. While many designs could work, the possibility shown here reflects the high stems which were a hallmark of ancient ships.

2. A window

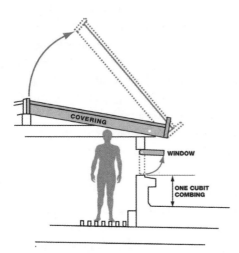

Any opening on the deck of a ship needs a wall (combing) to prevent water from flowing in, especially when the ship rolls. In this illustration, the window "ends a cubit upward and above," as described in Genesis 6:16. The central position of the skylight is chosen to reflect the idea of a "noon light." This also means that the window does not need to be exactly one cubit. Perhaps the skylight had a transparent roof (even more a "noon light"), or the skylight roof could be opened (which might correspond to when "Noah removed the covering of the Ark"). While variations are possible, a window without combing is not the most logical solution.

3. Mortise and tenon planking

Ancient shipbuilders usually began with a shell of planks (strakes) and then built internal framing (ribs) to fit inside. This is the complete reverse of the familiar European method where planking was added to the frame. In shell-first construction, the planks must be attached to each other somehow. Some used overlapping (clinker) planks that were dowelled or nailed, others used rope to sew the planks together. The ancient Greeks used a sophisticated system where the planks were interlocked with thousands of precise mortise and tenon joints. The resulting hull was strong enough to

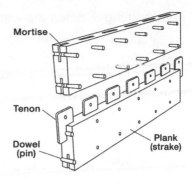

ram another ship, yet light enough to be hauled onto a beach by the crew. If this is what the Greeks could do centuries before Christ, what could Noah do centuries after Tubal-Cain invented forged metal tools?

4. Ramps

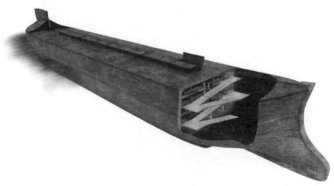

Ramps help to get animals and heavy loads between decks. Running them across the hull avoids cutting through important deck beams, and this location is away from the middle of the hull where bending stresses are highest. (This placement also better utilizes the irregular space at bow and stern.)

5. Something to catch the water

To assist in turning the Ark to point with the wind, the stern should resist being pushed sideways. This is the same as a fixed rudder or skeg that provides directional control. There are many ways this could be done, but here we are reflecting the "mysterious" stern extensions seen on the earliest large ships of the Mediterranean.

Was Noah's Ark the biggest ship ever built?

Few wooden ships have ever come close to the size of Noah's Ark. One possible challenge comes from the Chinese treasure ships of Yung He in the 1400s. An older contender is the ancient Greek trireme *Tessaronteres*.

At first historians dismissed ancient Greek claims that the *Tessaronteres* was 425 feet (130 m) long. But as more information was learned, the reputation of these early shipbuilders grew markedly. One of the greatest challenges to the construction of large wooden ships is finding a way to lay planks around the outside in a way that will ensure little or no leaking, which is caused when there is too much movement between the planks. Apparently, the Greeks had access to an extraordinary method of planking that was lost for centuries, and only recently brought to light by marine archaeology.

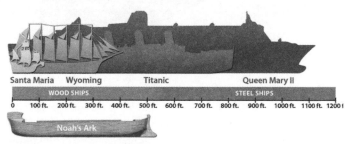

How big was the Ark? It depends on your cubit size! To get the 510 feet (155 m) given here, we used a cubit of 20.4 inches (51.8 cm). This diagram shows how Noah's Ark compares to other large ships.

It is not known when or where this technique originated. Perhaps they used a method that began with the Ark. After all, if the Greeks could do it, why not Noah?

The Ark is near the maximum size that is known to be possible for a wooden vessel.

---

1. Other objects spoken of in Scripture lack physical details which have been discovered (through archaeology and other research) later (e.g., the walls of Jericho were actually double and situated on a hillside—one higher than the other with a significant space of several feet between them).

2. C. Cohen, "Hebrew TBH: Proposed Etymologies," *The Journal of the Ancient Near Eastern Society (JANES)*, (1972): 36–51. (The journal was at that time called *The Journal of the Ancient Near Eastern Society of Columbia University*, Ancient Near Eastern Society of Columbia University, New York.)

Mything the Boat

by Dan Lietha

Noah's Ark is not just an old sea vessel floating alone in the pages of the Bible—it's a modern marketing extravaganza! Images of Noah's Ark—mostly directed at children—are everywhere: on fine art prints, children's books, wallpaper, toys, tapestries, greeting cards, T-shirts, magazine and TV ads, posters, wall decorations, and even business logos. And these images are not just aimed at the "religious" market; they are also hot items among the secular crowd.

Have you ever stopped to think how the Ark—such a powerful reminder of God's judgment—became so popular, considering the rejection of the true account of Noah's Flood by so many?

It can't be because of what the Ark really stands for. The Bible says that people are willingly ignorant that "the world that then was, being overflowed with water, perished" (2 Peter 3:5–6, KJV).

A clue to the Ark's popularity can be found in the Ark images themselves.

Redesigners of the lost Ark

Most Ark images bear little resemblance to the one described in Genesis. Artists generally ignore the information in Scripture in favor of a wide variety of imaginative shapes, sizes, and themes. The most common version is a toy-like boat, stuffed full of cuddly animals that crowd around Noah. Why is that?

Some artists treat the Ark like an amusing myth or children's fairy tale. They do not believe that the story is an account of actual events, and therefore they have no problem in doing anything they want with it.

Even artists and companies who believe the Bible's account of Noah's Flood sometimes choose to create a caricature of the Ark for artistic and sales reasons. For instance, small arks take less to time to draw, are cute, sell well, and make it easy to show the entire Ark and animals in one scene. And small arks aren't controversial, either, because they don't look real.

An Ark of biblical proportions

In addition to a lack of accuracy, the modern arks have a more serious drawback. One of the most-asked questions about Noah's Ark is how Noah fit all the animals into it. The size of the Ark is critical to the believability of the biblical account, and so is a realistic shape that could survive the Flood. Yet the Ark images that come to most people's minds fall far short.

In our modern, media-saturated culture, it is true that seeing is believing, especially for young children. Images make a strong impression and often overshadow the biblical account, even for those who have a moderate familiarity with whatever event is being described. So while airplanes and other well-known objects may be fine to caricature, promoting poor caricatures of the Ark can be harmful.

Sadly, with the best of intentions, the Church has promoted cutesy caricatures of the Ark in Sunday school materials and other literature, leaving the world largely unaware of the real message of the Ark that God instructed Noah to build.

The Bible explains why the modern world is willingly ignorant. It's because they don't want to face the reality that judgment is coming again: "But the heavens and the earth, which are now preserved by the same word, are reserved for fire until the day of judgment and perdition of ungodly men" (2 Peter 3:7).

CARTOONS—THEY CAN ACCURATELY DEPICT TRUTH

The cartoon ark (above) is an example of how Noah's Ark is commonly misrepresented. However, the problem does not lie in cartooning as a form of illustration, but rather the degree of distortion applied in the specific cartoon. For example, when the same distorted cartoon ark is depicted in a realistic setting (below, top), the picture remains an absurd portrayal of Noah's Ark. However, a cartoonist can draw the Ark in a way that reflects the true size and dimensions of the boat described in Genesis (below, bottom). Cartoons can be a very effective way to communicate accurate truth to all ages.

Dan Lietha, cartoonist and illustrator for AiG, graduated from the Joe Kubert School of Cartoon and Graphic Art. Some of his projects include *After Eden* and the *Creationwise* comic strip. He has also illustrated the book *When Dragons' Hearts Were Good* and the *Answers for Kids* curricula.

Caring for the Animals on the Ark

by John Woodmorappe

*A*ccording to Scripture, Noah's Ark was a safe haven for representatives of all the kinds of air-breathing land animals that God created. While it is possible that God made miraculous provisions for the daily care of these animals, it is not necessary—or required by Scripture—to appeal to miracles. Exploring natural solutions for day-to-day operations does not discount God's role: the biblical account hints at plenty of miracles as written, such as God bringing the animals to the Ark (Genesis 6:20; 7:9, 15). It turns out that a study of existing, low-tech animal care methods answers trivial objections to the Ark. In fact, many solutions to seemingly insurmountable problems are rather straightforward.

How did Noah fit all the animals on the Ark?

According to the Bible, the Ark had three decks (floors). It is not difficult to show that there was plenty of room for 16,000 animals (the maximum number of animals on the Ark, if the most liberal approach to counting animals is applied), assuming they required approximately the same floor space as animals in typical farm enclosures and laboratories. The vast majority of the creatures (birds, reptiles, and mammals) were small (the largest only a few hundred pounds of body weight). What's more, many could have been housed in groups, which would have further reduced the required space.

It is still necessary to take account of the floor spaces required by large animals, such as elephants and rhinos. But even these, collectively, do not require a large area because it is most likely that these animals were young, but not newborns. Even the largest dinosaurs were relatively small when only a few years old.

What did the dinosaurs eat?

Dinosaurs could have eaten basically the same foods as the other animals. The large sauropods could have eaten compressed hay, other dried plant material, seeds and grains, and the like. Carnivorous dinosaurs—if any were meat-eaters before the Flood—could have eaten dried meat, reconstituted dried meat, or slaughtered animals. Giant tortoises would have been ideal to use as food in this regard. They were large and needed little food to be maintained themselves. There are also exotic sources of meat, such as fish that wrap themselves in dry cocoons.

It is not necessary—or required by Scripture—to appeal to miracles for the provision and daily care of the animals on the Ark. Many solutions to seemingly insurmountable problems are rather straightforward.

How were the animals cared for?

We must distinguish between the long-term care required for animals kept in zoos and the temporary, emergency care required on the Ark. The animals' comfort and healthy appearance were not essential for emergency survival during one stressful year, where survival was the primary goal.

Studies of nonmechanized animal care indicate that eight people could have fed and watered 16,000 creatures. The key is to avoid unnecessary walking around. As the old adage says, "Don't work harder, work smarter."

Therefore, Noah probably stored the food and water near each animal. Even better, drinking water could have been piped into troughs, just as the Chinese have used bamboo pipes for this purpose for thousands of years. The use of some sort of self-feeders, as is commonly done for birds, would have been relatively easy and probably essential. Animals that required special care or diets were uncommon and should not have needed an inordinate amount of time from the handlers. Even animals with the most specialized diets in nature could have been switched to readily sustainable substitute diets. Of course, this assumes that animals with specialized diets today were likewise specialized at the time of the Flood.

How did the animals breathe?

Based on my two decades of research, I do not believe that anything more was needed than a basic, non-mechanical ventilation system. The density of animals on the Ark, compared to the volume of enclosed space, was much less than we find in some modern, mass animal housing used to keep stock raised for food (such as chicken farms), which requires no special mechanical ventilation.

It is reasonable to believe that one relatively small window would have adequately ventilated the Ark. Of course if there were a window along the top center section, which the Bible allows, all occupants would be even more comfortable. It is also interesting to note that

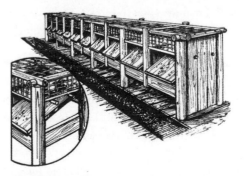

Animal enclosures with sloped, self-cleaning floors, emptying into a manure gutter or pit.

the convective movement of air, driven by temperature differences between the warm-blooded animals and the cold interior surfaces, would have been significant enough to drive the flow of air. Plus, wind blowing into the window would have enhanced the ventilation further. However, if supplementary ventilation was necessary, it could have been provided by wave motion, fire thermal, or even a small number of animals harnessed to slow-moving rotary fans.

What did Noah and his family do with the animal waste?

As much as 12 U.S. tons (11 metric tons) of animal waste may have been produced daily. The key to keeping the enclosures clean was to avoid the need for Noah and his family to do the work. The right systems could also prevent the need to change animal bedding. Noah could have accomplished this in several ways. One possibility would be to allow the waste to accumulate below the animals, much as we see in modern pet shops. In this regard, there could have been slatted floors, and animals could have trampled their waste into the pits below. Small animals, such as birds, could have multiple levels in their enclosures, and waste could have simply accumulated at the bottom of each.

The danger of toxic or explosive manure gases, such as methane, would be alleviated by the constant movement of the Ark, which would have allowed manure gases to be constantly released. Secondly, methane, which is half the density of air, would quickly find its way out of a small opening such as a window. There is no reason to believe that the levels of these gases within the Ark would have approached hazardous levels.

Alternatively, sloped floors would have allowed the waste to flow into large central gutters. Noah's family could have then dumped this overboard without an excessive expenditure of manpower.

The problem of manure odor may, at first thought, seem insurmountable. But we must remember that, throughout most of human history, humans lived together with their farm animals. Barns, separate from human living quarters, are a relatively recent development.

While the voyage of the Ark may not have been comfortable or easy, it was certainly doable, even under such unprecedented circumstances.

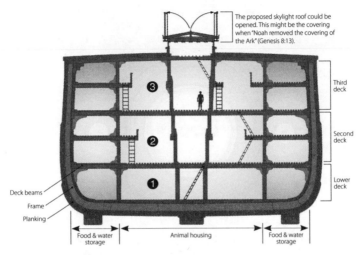

The proposed skylight roof could be opened. This might be the covering when "Noah removed the covering of the Ark" (Genesis 8:13).

Third deck

Second deck

Lower deck

Deck beams
Frame
Planking

Food & water storage   Animal housing   Food & water storage

A look inside the Ark: This is a cross-section view of a possible design of the interior of the Ark.

Three decks

Genesis 6:16 instructs that the Ark is to be made "with lower, second, and third decks." In this version of the Ark's interior, there are two levels that do not extend across the entire width of the ship. These half-floors are not separate levels.

Animal housing

Genesis 6:14 instructs Noah to "make rooms [nests] in the

This scale model shows the effective design of Noah's Ark. This second-floor model shows the extra half-floor within the three deck structure that could have been used for possible storage or animal housing.

Model created by Tim Foley.

ark." These rooms or nests would simply be stalls and cages for the animals.

Stairs

Several staircases and ladders could be fitted throughout the Ark to gain quick access to another deck. Ramps near the ends of the hull (as seen in Chapter 3: Thinking Outside the Box) could be used to get animals and heavy loads between decks.

Food & water

Mezzanine levels improve access to food storage, utilizing gravity to supply grain and water to the animal enclosures below. Water could be directed in pipes (metal, wood, leather, bamboo, etc.) from tanks on upper levels.

Light & ventilation

The central skylight provides lighting and ventilation to the center section of the Ark. Slatted floors maximize airflow to the lower decks.

John Woodmorappe has been a researcher in the areas of biology, geology, and paleontology for over twenty years. He has two BA degrees and an MA in geology. John has also been a public school science teacher.

Has Noah's Ark Been Found?

by John Morris

The ancient Greek historian Herodotus mentioned that religious pilgrims journeyed to Mt. Ararat, which traditionally has been accepted as the landing place of Noah's Ark. The Armenian people, who have lived at the foot of Ararat since before the time of Christ, maintain a strong attachment to Noah and the Ark.

In recent centuries, interest in the mountain and the huge wooden boat that may rest there has spread. Adventurous mountain-climbing Europeans first conquered the 17,000-foot (5,182-meter) summit in 1829. Reports in the twentieth century of wood being found high above the treeline fueled intense interest in new expeditions. Most notably, French explorer Fernando Navarro claimed in 1955 to have discovered wooden timbers in a glacial crevasse, stimulating even more interest among Western Christians, including me as a little boy.

Mt. Ararat, which is traditionally thought to be the landing place of the Ark, is located in eastern Turkey near the border with Armenia and Iran.

Many questioned Navarro's find, but in 1969 a carefully planned expedition, with Navarro as a guide, discovered only another controversial piece of supposed wood. Yet excitement continues today, fueled by hopes of discovering a mostly intact ship—or at least indisputable remnants—high on this or another mountain in the Ararat range.

The modern search

The modern search for the Ark actually commenced with Eryl Cummings in the 1940s when he began to gather anecdotal evidence of sightings. He and colleagues made several trips to Ararat to explore and study this remote mountain in the Muslim nation of Turkey. His 1972 book *Noah's Ark: Fact or Fable* captivated the imagination of those who read it. Soon several expedition teams trekked to Mt. Ararat, including my own.

The newly formed Institute for Creation Research sponsored my first expedition in 1972. While our group of five strong climbers and photographers didn't find the Ark, we gathered new climbing details and an abundance of photographs and notes regarding the topography. As a result, the search grew in earnest.

I've journeyed thirteen times to Ararat, as others have done, including the now-deceased Apollo astronaut Jim Irwin. These

Climbing along a steep ridgeline of loose glacial skree during one of thirteen expeditions to Ararat led by Dr. John Morris

Photo courtesy Dr. John Morris

trips have met with danger and varying success in helping to narrow the field of search. Not only is the mountain high and treacherous, but wild animals, intense storms, local bandits, and government opposition have been very real impediments. In recent years, Kurdish insurgents have used the mountain as a staging ground for terrorism throughout Turkey, as well as nearby Syria and Iraq.

The early expeditions were all on foot, with mountaineers doing their best to cover the huge mountain. Most of the efforts hoped for a visual sighting, but some used ground-penetrating sonar, ice-cutting equipment, infrared scanners, and GPS positioning. On several occasions aircraft were permitted, both fixed-wing and helicopter. Obviously, many more sites could be investigated from the air than on foot. The entire mountain has even been photographed in stereo, yet without a confirmed sighting.

In addition to the scientific and archaeological significance, the Ark's discovery would awaken new discussion about God's wrath and His provision of a route to restoration.

Surely, after all this study we would know whether the Ark is on Ararat. But the mountain changes every year, revealing previously veiled secrets. Winter snows, shifting glaciers, and rock and ice avalanches expose and hide what lies underneath. Even after one site has been investigated thoroughly, it needs to be revisited. Many possible sites have been ruled out, but currently there are several "hot spots" that I and others would like to check.

In addition to expeditions that gather first-hand information, researchers continue to gather eyewitness testimony from individuals who claim to have seen the Ark. Their descriptions are substantially the same. According to numerous supposed eyewitnesses, something is up there, and the shape and composition they describe fits the biblical description and dimensions.

Hindering the search are false and even fraudulent accounts that embarrass serious searchers. Many have rushed to make claims with supposed evidence that cannot stand up to scrutiny. Yet, public fascination continues. Many people think the resting place and remnants of the Ark have already been found. But where is the physical evidence? We have a lot of smoke, but no fire.

The general consensus among most biblical creationists is that Mt. Ararat is the resting place for Noah's Ark. However, certain factors weaken this claim. Consider the following points both for and against Mount Ararat as the final resting place of the Ark. Photo courtesy NASA

On Mount Ararat

The name "Ararat," for the Turkish name "Agri Dagi," is probably based on the Hebrew "rrt" in Genesis.

Its location is high, allowing the Ark to land before the "tops of the mountains were seen" (Genesis 8:5).

Based on eyewitness reports, few other places could hide the Ark in ice for 4,300 years—if such preservation were even possible.

On Another Mountain

Ararat is a volcanic cone with little evidence that it was ever under water during the Flood, indicating that it may have formed after the Flood.

As they left the Ark, the animals would have had to make their way down a 16,950 feet (5,165 m) volcano.

Noah reported distant ranges without mentioning the closer Lesser Ararat.

The Bible reveals only that "the Ark rested . . . on the mountains of Ararat" (Genesis 8:4). That's a sizable *region*, not a mountain. Several locations have been proposed, including some in Iran and southern Turkey. However, the numerous eyewitness accounts seem to me and others to best point to the modern Mt. Ararat, and it is for this reason most expeditions focus there. Indeed, the only reason to search at all is that some claim to have seen it. A select few say that they have touched it, looked inside it, even recovered but later lost actual wood from the site. The Bible does not mention its survival or discovery. In my view, because of the glaciers, earthquakes, and other onslaughts of nature, the Ark could not have survived without God's supernatural protection.

Inscriptions on a ruined structure dating to early Christian times, possibly commemorating a nearby altar.

Photo courtesy Dr. John Morris

The possible significance

A well-documented and scientifically viable discovery would be quite newsworthy, and it is exciting to consider how it might impact world culture.

A successful discovery would impact several fields of study. Archaeologically, it would affirm and excite the faith of Christians, giving them a bit more understanding of the world that Noah's Flood (actually, God's Flood!) was sent to obliterate. Scientifically, it would challenge the assumption that earth conditions are generally constant over time, which is an underlying assumption of evolution and naturalism. Since the Ark is a beautiful picture of Jesus Christ, and the Flood is a horrible reminder of the penalty for sin, the Ark's discovery would awaken new discussion about God's wrath and His provision of a route to restoration, and escape from the judgment that is to come.

Questionable claims of Ark discoveries blunt the potential impact of a true discovery. But I am convinced and sincerely pray that if found, the Ark will once again warn a rebellious world of the judgment to come. For this reason—on Mt. Ararat and throughout the mountains of that region—I think the search should go on.

John Morris earned his BS in civil engineering from Virginia Polytechnic Institute and an MS and PhD in geological engineering from the University of Oklahoma. He is president of the Institute for Creation Research and wrote *Is the Big Bang Biblical?* and numerous children's books.

Noah the Evangelist

by Paul F. Taylor and Gary Vaterlaus

Christians have gleaned many valuable lessons from Noah and the Ark. But one fact is often overlooked. He was the first evangelist mentioned in the Bible. Are there any lessons his life can teach us about how to present the gospel? Absolutely!

For one, Noah faced the same circumstances that Christians face today.

"As the days of Noah were, so also will the coming of the Son of Man be. For as in the days before the flood, they were eating and drinking, marrying and giving in marriage, until the day that Noah entered the ark, and did not know until the flood came and took them all away, so also will the coming of the Son of Man be" (Matthew 24:36–39).

A certain future

The analogy is very instructive. Just as most people today do not believe Jesus is coming back at all, let alone soon, the people of Noah's day did not know when the Flood was going to happen. However, they were informed that there was indeed going to be a Flood. Their information came from many sources:

1. from the fact that Noah was actually building an Ark.
2. from the warning of God's Spirit (Genesis 6:3 says, "And the Lord said, 'My Spirit shall not strive with man forever, for he is indeed flesh; yet his days shall be one hundred and twenty years.'").
3. quite likely, from the words of Noah himself.

Like people today, almost certainly the people of Noah's day were busy enjoying the pleasures of life and did not believe or care that judgment was coming.

During the decades of mankind's last days, Noah was working on the Ark. As it grew, it must have been a potent symbol to those living nearby. One can imagine that Noah was often asked about his construction project. Indeed, it is likely that he was mocked for such an enterprise.

A silent preacher and his faith

In 2 Peter 2:5, Noah is described as a "preacher of righteousness." In what way was he a preacher? The Greek word *kerux* (κηρυξ) refers to a herald, or "one who announces." Even when he wasn't saying anything, his labor on the Ark would have been his witness. However, some Jewish scholars maintain that Noah did indeed leave some words, too. John Gill, in chapter 22 of the *Pirke R. Eliezer*, quotes Noah's words according to Jewish tradition: "Be ye turned from your evil ways and works, lest the waters of the flood come upon you, and cut off all the seed of the children of men."

The tradition shows Noah giving both a warning and a means of salvation. If this extrabiblical source has any truth in it, then Noah is asking for people to repent, which would certainly fit with his own source of salvation through Christ. Noah was not saved because of his righteousness—at least not in a worldly sense. Hebrews 11 tells us from where Noah's righteousness came. The Greek word is *dikaiosune* (δικαιοσύνη), which refers to a form of righteousness that is unattainable by law or by merit.

Hebrews 11:7 says, "By faith Noah, being divinely warned of things not yet seen, moved with godly fear, prepared an ark for the saving of his household, by which he condemned the world and became heir of the righteousness which is according to faith."

This sort of righteousness is found only by faith. The Apostle

Paul says elsewhere, "For by grace you have been saved through faith, and that not of yourselves; it is the gift of God, not of works, lest anyone should boast" (Ephesians 2:8–9).

This is exactly how Noah was saved. His righteousness was unattainable; so it could only come by God's grace, through faith. Genesis 6:8 tells us that "Noah found grace in the eyes of the Lord." Noah's salvation, like ours, was by grace. He could not do anything to attain righteousness for himself.

An available safety

In His instructions for building the Ark, God told Noah to "set the door of the Ark in its side" (Genesis 6:16). The Ark had only one door to pass through to escape God's terrible judgment. By faith, Noah and his family entered the Ark. Once they were all inside, the Lord shut them in (Genesis 7:16).

What is significant about God shutting the door of the Ark? It provides a wonderful demonstration of the twin truths of man's responsibility and God's sovereignty that we see throughout Scripture.

When the door to the Ark was shut, there was room for many more people. All they had to do was repent and turn to God. In the same way, salvation is available to "whoever calls on the name of the Lord" (Romans 10:13). Notice that the eight occupants of the Ark entered by a door—and there was only one door—which was not closed by Noah, but by God—"the Lord shut him in" (Genesis 7:16). Jesus said, "I am the door. If anyone enters by Me, he will be saved" (John 10:9). The Ark pictures salvation in Jesus Christ, our "Ark" of salvation.

The willing Savior

Noah's Flood teaches us two things about the attitude of God toward us.

He is angry with sin and will punish it one day.

He loves us and sends us a way of salvation, if we will only repent and turn to Him.

Jesus is our Ark of Salvation today. Just as Noah was saved by grace through faith from the destruction of the Flood, we can be saved by grace through faith in Jesus, when we repent and turn to Him.

The Bible makes it clear that we are "dead in trespasses and sins" (Ephesians 2:1). Nothing we can do can save us from our sin and its consequence of eternal separation from God. But the Bible also tells us that if we confess with our mouth the Lord Jesus and believe in our heart that God has raised Him from the dead, we will be saved (Romans 10:9). It is "by grace you have been saved through faith, and that not of yourselves; it is the gift of God" (Ephesians 2:8). Nothing we can do will save us from our sin—salvation is all of God. Yet our responsibility is to go through the doorway (Jesus), and God will save us.

All Christians, just as Noah, have a responsibility to share the message of salvation with a world that is perishing. The lessons from the account of Noah are a great reminder of that truth.

Paul F. Taylor graduated with his BSc. in chemistry from Nottingham University and his masters in science education from Cardiff University. Paul taught science for 17 years in a state school and is now a proficient writer and speaker for Answers in Genesis–UK.

Gary Vaterlaus earned his undergraduate and master's degrees in science education from Oregon State University. He also studied at Western Conservative Baptist Seminary. He is director of curriculum development for Answers in Genesis–USA.

How Did Animals Spread All Over the World?

by Paul F. Taylor

An issue often used in an attempt to beat biblical creationists over the head is the worldwide distribution of animals. Such a distribution, say critics, proves that there could never have been a global Flood or an Ark. If the Ark landed somewhere in the Middle East, then all the animals would have disembarked at that point, including animals that we do not find in the Middle East today, or in the fossil record in that area. How did kangaroos get to Australia, or kiwis to New Zealand? How did polar bears get to North America and penguins to Antarctica?

Not a science textbook

Skeptics often claim, "The Bible is not a science textbook." This, of course, is true—because science textbooks change every year, whereas the Bible is the unchanging Word of God—the God who cannot lie. Nevertheless, the Bible can be relied upon when it touches on every scientific issue, including ecology. It is the Bible that gives us the big picture. Within this big picture, we can build scientific models that help us explain how past events may have come about. Such models should be held to lightly, but the Scripture to which they refer is inerrant. That is to say future research may cast doubt on an actual model, without casting doubt on Scripture.

With this in mind, the question needs to be asked, "Is there a Bible-based model that we can use to help explain how animals might have migrated from where the Ark landed to where they live today?" The answer is yes.

The hard facts

A biblical model of animal migration obviously must start with the Bible. From Genesis we can glean the following pertinent facts:

1. "And of every living thing of all flesh you shall bring two of every sort into the ark, to keep them alive with you; they shall be male and female. Of the birds after their kind, of animals after their kind, and of every creeping thing of the earth after its kind, two of every kind will come to you to keep them alive" (Genesis 6:19–20). The Bible is clear that representatives of all the *kinds* of air-breathing land animals and birds were present on the Ark. A technical term used by some creation scientists for these *kinds* is *baramin*—derived from the Hebrew words for *created kind*. Within these baramins is all the information necessary to produce all current species. For example, it is unlikely that the Ark contained two lions and two tigers. It is more likely that it contained two feline animals, from which lions, tigers, and other cat-like creatures have developed.

2. Another lesson from Genesis 6:20 is that the animals came to Noah. He did not have to go and catch them. Therefore, this preservation of the world's fauna was divinely controlled. It was God's intention that the fauna be preserved. The animals' recolonization of the land masses was therefore determined by God, and not left to chance.

3. "Then the ark rested in the seventh month, the seventeenth day of the month, on the mountains of Ararat" (Genesis 8:4). The Bible is clear that the Ark landed in the region of Ararat,

but much debate has ensued over whether this is the same region as the locality of the present-day mountain known as Ararat. This issue is of importance, as we shall see. The Bible uses the plural "mountains." It is unlikely that the Ark rested on a point on the top of a mountain, in the manner often illustrated in children's picture books. Rather, the landing would have been among the mountainous areas of eastern Turkey, where present-day Mount Ararat is located, and western Iran, where the range extends.

4. It was God's will that the earth be recolonized. "Then God spoke to Noah, saying, 'Go out of the ark, you and your wife, and your sons and your sons' wives with you. Bring out with you every living thing of all flesh that is with you: birds and cattle and every creeping thing that creeps on the earth, so that they may abound on the earth, and be fruitful and multiply on the earth.' So Noah went out, and his sons and his wife and his sons' wives with him. Every animal, every creeping thing, every bird, and whatever creeps on the earth, according to their families, went out of the ark" (Genesis 8:15–19). The abundance and multiplication of the animals was also God's will.

The biblical principles that we can establish then are that, after the Flood, God desired the ecological reconstruction of the world, including its vulnerable animal kinds, and the animals must have spread out from a mountainous region known as Ararat.

The construction of any biblical model of recolonization must include these principles. The model suggested on the following pages is constructed in good faith, to explain the observed facts through the "eyeglasses" of the Bible. The Bible is inspired, but our scientific models are not. If we subsequently find the model to be untenable, this would not shake our commitment to the absolute authority of Scripture.

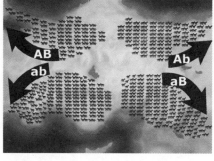

The model uses the multiplication of dogs as an example of how animals could have quickly repopulated the earth. Two dogs came off Noah's Ark and began breeding more dogs. Within a relatively short time period, there would be an incredible number of dogs of all sorts of different shapes and sizes.

These dogs then began to spread out from the Ararat region to all parts of the globe.

As these dogs spread around the world, variations within the dog kind led to many of the varieties we find today. But it is important to note that they are still dogs. This multiplication of variations within a kind is the same with the many other kinds of animals.

One final comment must be made in this section. As I have used the word recolonization several times, I must emphasize that I am not referring to the so-called *Recolonization Theory*. This theory will be discussed later.

Modern recolonizations

One accusation thrown at biblical creationists is that kangaroos could not have hopped to Australia, because there are no fossils of kangaroos on the way. But the expectation of such fossils is a presuppositional error. Such an expectation is predicated on the assumption that fossils form gradually and inevitably from animal populations. In fact, fossilization is by no means inevitable. It usually requires sudden, rapid burial. Otherwise the bones would decompose before permineralization. One ought likewise to ask why it is that, despite the fact that millions of bison used to roam the prairies of North America, hardly any bison fossils are found there. Similarly, lion fossils are not found in Israel even though we know that lions once lived there.

Comparisons can be made with more modern recolonizations. For example, the *Encyclopædia Britannica* has the following to say about Surtsey Island and Krakatoa and the multiplication of species.

> Six months after the eruption of a volcano on the island of Surtsey off the coast of Iceland in 1963, the island had been colonized by a few bacteria, molds, insects, and birds. Within about a year of the eruption of a volcano on the island of Krakatoa in the tropical Pacific in 1883, a few grass species, insects, and vertebrates had taken hold. On both Surtsey and Krakatoa, only a few decades had elapsed before hundreds of species reached the islands. Not all species are able to take hold and become permanently established, but eventually the island communities stabilize into a dynamic equilibrium.[1]

There is little secret, therefore, how nonflying animals may have traveled to the outer parts of the world after the Flood. Many of them could have floated on vast floating logs, left-overs from the massive pre-Flood forests that were ripped up during the Flood and likely remained afloat for many decades on the world's oceans, transported by world currents. Others could later have been taken by people. Savolainen et al., have suggested, for example, that all Australian dingoes are descended from a single female domesticated dog from Southeast Asia.[2] A third explanation of possible later migration is that animals could have crossed land bridges. This is, after all, how it is supposed by evolutionists that many animals and people migrated from Asia to the Americas—over a land bridge at the Bering Straits. For such land bridges to have existed, we may need to assume that sea levels were lower in the post-Flood period—an assumption based on a biblical model of the Ice Age.

Ice Age

As Michael Oard, a retired meteorologist and Ice Age researcher, has suggested, an Ice Age may have followed closely after the Flood. In his detailed analysis, Oard proposed a mechanism of how the rare conditions required to form an Ice Age may have been triggered by the Flood, and shows how this explains the field evidence for an Ice Age.[3]

Severe climatic changes could have been the catalyst that encouraged certain species to migrate in certain directions. These severe changes could also have accounted for some of the many extinctions that occurred. Additionally, Oard's studies provide a model for how land bridges could have developed.

Oard has pointed out that certain observed features from the Ice Age cause problems for the evolutionist, not the creationist. Thus, a creationist explanation of the Ice Age better explains the facts. An example of such an issue is that of disharmonious associations of fossils—fossils of creatures normally associated with different conditions (such as creatures with a preference for hot and cold climates) being found in close proximity.

One of the more puzzling problems for uniformitarian theories of the ice age is disharmonious associations of fossils, in which species from different climatic regimes are juxtaposed. For example, a hippopotamus fossil found together with a reindeer fossil.[4]

Oard suggests that even with present topography, a number of significant land bridges would have existed to facilitate migrations if the sea level were only 180 feet (55 m) below current levels. However, there is even evidence that the land in some places where land bridges would be necessary could have been higher still. Thus, land bridges facilitated by the Ice Age constitute a serious model to explain how some migrations could have been possible.

Some still remain skeptical about the idea of land bridges all the way to Australia. Nevertheless, by a combination of methods that we see today, including land bridges, there are rational explanations as to how animals may have reached the far corners of the world. Of course, we were not there at the time to witness how this migration may have happened, but those adhering to a biblical worldview can be certain that animals obviously did get to far places, and that there are rational ways in which it could have happened.

We should therefore have no problem accepting the Bible as true. Creationist scientific models of animal migration are equally as valid as evolutionary models, if not more so. The reason such models are rejected is that they do not fit in with the orthodox, secular evolutionary worldview.

It is not a problem for us to rationalize why certain animals do not appear in certain parts of the world. Why, for example, does Australia have such an unusual fauna, including so many marsupials? Marsupials are, of course, known elsewhere in the world. For example, opossums are found in North and South America, and fossilized marsupials have been found elsewhere. But in many places, climatic changes and other factors could lead to their extinction.

The lack of great marsupials in other continents need be no more of a problem than the lack of dinosaurs. As with many species today, they just died out—a reminder of a sin-cursed world. One proposed theory is that marsupials—because they bore their young in pouches—were able to travel farther and faster than mammals that had to stop to care for their young. They were able to establish themselves in far-flung Australia before competitors reached the continent.

Similar statements could be made about the many unusual bird species in New Zealand, on islands from which mammals were absent until the arrival of European settlers.

Recolonization theory

The most logical interpretation of the biblical record of the Flood and its aftermath would seem to suggest that the animals disembarked and then recolonized the planet. Comparisons with modern migrations and incidents such as Surtsey have suggested that this recolonization need not have taken long. A plain reading of Scripture suggests that the Ark landed in the mountains of Ararat, most likely in the region of modern Turkey and Central Asia. It is also our contention that the significant quantity of death represented by the fossil record is best understood by reference to the Genesis Flood (i.e., the majority of fossils formed as a result of the Flood).

More recently, a theory has developed among certain creationists in the UK and Europe which suggests that the fossil record is actually a record not of catastrophe but of processes occurring during recolonization. This theory is called the Recolonization Theory.[5]

Proponents of this theory suggest that the Flood completely obliterated the earth's previous crust so that none of the present fossils were caused by it. To accommodate fossilization processes, Recolonization Theory suggests that the age of the earth be stretched by a few thousand years. Some advocates of this view suggest an age of about 8,000 years for the earth, while others suggest figures as high as 20,000 years.

A detailed criticism of Recolonization Theory has previously been published by McIntosh, Edmondson, and Taylor[6], and another by Holt.[7]

The principal error of this view is that it starts from supposed scientific anomalies, such as the fossil record, rather than from Scripture. This has led to the proposals among some Recolonizers, but not all, that there must be gaps in the genealogies recorded in Genesis 5 and 11, even though there is no need for such gaps. Indeed the suggestion of gaps in these genealogies causes further doctrinal problems.[8]

Even the views of those Recolonizers who do not expand the genealogies contain possible seeds of compromise. Because the Recolonizers accept the geologic column, and because the Middle East has a great deal of what is called Cretaceous rock, it follows that the Middle East would need to be submerged after the Flood, at the very time of the Tower of Babel events in Genesis 11. This has led some of the Recolonizers to speculate that the Ark actually landed in Africa, and therefore, that continent was the host to the events of Genesis 11 and 12. This would seem to be a very weak position exegetically and historically. Such exegetical weaknesses led Professor Andy McIntosh and his colleagues to comment, "Their science is driving their interpretation of Scripture, and not the other way round."[9]

Conclusions

We must not be downhearted by critics and their frequent accusations against the Bible. We must not be surprised that so many people will believe all sorts of strange things, whatever the logic.

Starting from our presupposition that the Bible's account is true, we have seen that scientific models can be developed to explain the post-Flood migration of animals. These models correspond to observed data and are consistent with the Bible's account. It is notable that opponents of biblical creationism use similar models in their evolutionary explanations of animal migrations. While a model may eventually be superseded, it is important to note that such biblically consistent models exist. In any event, we have confidence in the scriptural account, finding it to be accurate and authoritative.[10] The fact of animal migration around the world is illustrative of the goodness and graciousness of God, who provided above and beyond our needs.

---

1. *Encyclopædia Britannica*, "Community Ecology," http://www.britannica.com/eb/article-70601.

2. P. Savolainen et al., "A detailed picture of the origin of the Australian dingo, obtained from the study of mitochondrial DNA," *PNAS* (Proceedings of the National Academy of Sciences of the United States of America) 101 (2004): 12387–12390.

3. Oard has published many articles in journals and on the AiG and ICR websites on these issues. For a detailed account of his findings, see his book: M. Oard, *An Ice Age Caused by the Genesis Flood* (El Cajon, CA: Institute for Creation Research, 2002).

4. Ibid, p. 80.

5. Spelled "Recolonisation" in the UK, which is where the theory began.

6. A.C. McIntosh, T. Edmondson, and S. Taylor, "Flood Models: The need for an integrated approach," *TJ* 14 no. 1 (2000): 52–59; A.C. McIntosh, T. Edmondson, and S. Taylor, "Genesis and Catastrophe," *TJ* 14 no. 1 (2000): 101–109. Recolonizers' disagreements with these articles were answered in A.C. McIntosh, T. Edmondson, and S. Taylor, "McIntosh, Taylor, and Edmondson reply to Flood Models," *TJ* 14 no. 3 (2000): 80–82, available online at www.answersingenesis.org/tj/v14/i3/flood_reply.asp.

7. R. Holt, "Evidence for a Late Cainozoic Flood/post-Flood Boundary," *TJ* 10 no. 1 (1996): 128–168.

8. For more on this, see www.answersingenesis.org/articles/am/v1/n2/who-begat-whom.

9. A.C. McIntosh, T. Edmondson, and S. Taylor, "McIntosh, Taylor, and Edmondson reply to Flood Models," *TJ* 14 no. 3 (2000): 80–82.

10. John Woodmorappe has documented various detailed scientific models pertaining to the Ark, pre-Flood, and post-Flood issues in his book *Noah's Ark: A Feasibility Study* (El Cajon, CA: Institute for Creation Research, 1996).

Taking Back the Rainbow

by Ken Ham

From my childhood days as a lad in Australia to my travels today as a speaker with Answers in Genesis, I've seen scores—probably hundreds—of these amazing multicolored arches. Whether seen from the back seat of the family station wagon as it bounced down a dirt road in rural Queensland, or the window seat of a jetliner flying over a storm below, these beautiful bows remind me of my parents' teaching of what the Bible says about God's purpose in giving us the rainbow.

Twisted truth

Rainbows have come to be identified as symbolic of three basic concepts:

Promises—Genesis 9 records God's promise to Noah that He would never again destroy all flesh with a global flood.

Creation—Folklore and regional legends position the rainbow a bit differently. For example, Australian Aborigine and American Indian legends link it to creation events, and the Chinese have a legend concerning the rainbow and the creation of their first emperor Fohi.

Bridges—The rainbow has also been used to represent a bridge from earth (from humans) to a brighter, happier place. For instance, Judy Garland's "Somewhere Over the Rainbow" represents connecting to a happier place. The New Age religious movement also uses the rainbow as a bridge.

The rainbow has been used as a sign of a new era and a symbol of peace, love, and freedom. Sadly, the colors of the rainbow are even used on a flag for the gay and lesbian movement.

A biblical covenant of grace

However, the true meaning of the rainbow is revealed in Genesis 9:12–15:

"This is the sign of the covenant which I make between Me and you, and every living creature that is with you, for perpetual generations: I set My rainbow in the cloud, and it shall be for the sign of the covenant between Me and the earth. It shall be, when I bring a cloud over the earth, that the rainbow shall be seen in the cloud; and I will remember My covenant which is between Me and you and every living creature of all flesh; the waters shall never again become a flood to destroy all flesh."

First, the covenant of the rainbow is between God and man and the animal kinds that were with Noah on the Ark: a promise that there would never be such an event again that would destroy all flesh on the land. As there have been many local floods since that time, this is obviously a promise there would never be another global flood to destroy all flesh.

The Bible states clearly that there will be a future, global judgment, but next time by fire, not water (2 Peter 3:10). Some commentators even suggest that the watery colors of the rainbow (the blue end of the spectrum) remind us of the destruction by water, and the fiery colors (the red end of the spectrum) of the coming destruction by fire.

Secondly, the rainbow is a covenant of grace. It is actually a symbol of Christ Himself.

When the secular world hears the account of Noah's global Flood, they often accuse God of being an ogre for bringing this terrible judgment on people. However, the God of the Bible is a God of infinite mercy and grace.

God told Noah to build an Ark to save representative land animal kinds and Noah's family. However, this Ark was much larger than needed for just these animals and this family. Just as Noah and his family had to go through the door to be saved, so others could have gone through that door to be saved. In fact, after the Ark was loaded, it stood for seven more days before God Himself shut the door—seven more days of grace. And I have no doubt that Noah preached from the doorway, imploring people to come in and be saved. Noah's Ark is actually a picture of salvation in Christ, as He is the door through which we need to go to be saved for eternity (John 10:9).

All need to be reminded that we sinned in Adam—we committed high treason against the God of creation. God is holy and pure—completely without sin. A holy God has to judge sin, but in His judgment, He also shows infinite mercy. When God judged sin with death in Genesis 3:19, He also promised a Savior (Genesis 3:15). God Himself, in the person of the second member of the Trinity, the Lord Jesus Christ, stepped into history, fully human and fully God, to be a man so He could pay the penalty for our sin. Through the shedding of His blood, He offers the free gift of salvation to all who will believe.

The Bible reveals to us that the rainbow is a symbol of Christ in Ezekiel 1:26–28. In Revelation 4:2–3, John saw Christ clothed with a cloud and a rainbow on His head.

As Bible scholar John Gill states concerning the rainbow, "As it has in it a variety of beautiful colors, it may represent Christ, who is full of grace and truth, and fairer than the children of men; and may be considered as a symbol of peace and reconciliation by him, whom God looks unto, and remembers the covenant of his grace he has made with him and his chosen ones in him; and who is the rainbow round about the throne of God, and the way of access unto it."[1]

The next time you see a rainbow, remember that God judges sin. But He is also merciful, and He made a covenant of grace with Noah and the animals—He will never again judge with a worldwide Flood.

A reminder for all of us

So the next time you see a rainbow, remember that God judges sin. He judged with a global flood at the time of Noah. But He is merciful, and He made a covenant of grace with Noah and the animals that He would never again judge with a worldwide Flood. Not only that, but the rainbow, as a symbol of Christ, reminds us that He is the mediator between man and God and that those who receive the free gift of salvation are presented faultless before their Creator.

God declares those redeemed who have trusted in Christ. They are clothed in the righteousness of His Son. For the redeemed, the wrath of God toward sin was satisfied on the Cross—paid in full by the shed blood of His sinless Son.

And as John Gill puts it, "Though it is a bow, yet without arrows, and is not turned downwards towards the earth, but upwards towards heaven, and so is a token of mercy and kindness, and not of wrath and anger."[1]

I'm so thankful for a mum and dad who used what opportunities they had to instill in my siblings and me the truths of Scripture. Yes, we need to take the meaning of the rainbow back, and use it to tell the world of the mercy and kindness of our Creator and Savior, just like my mum and dad told me.

---

1.   *John Gill's Exposition of the Entire Bible*, adapted from Online Bible by Larry Pierce.

The Ark & the Gospel

As we ponder the scriptural account of Noah and the Ark, we cannot help but recognize God's judgment as the reason for the Flood. Many will take exception to the idea of a loving God wiping out the entire population of the earth, except for eight people. But that is exactly what is revealed in God's own words recorded by the pen of Moses. In Genesis 6:5–7 we read:

> Then the LORD saw that the wickedness of man was great in the earth, and that every intent of the thoughts of his heart was only evil continually. And the LORD was sorry that He had made man on the earth, and He was grieved in His heart. So the LORD said, "I will destroy man whom I have created from the face of the earth, both man and beast, creeping thing and birds of the air, for I am sorry that I have made them."

But the sin of mankind did not start here—it had escalated to this point. Adam and Eve chose to rebel against God's command in the Garden of Eden. They willfully ate of the forbidden fruit and brought sin into the human race. This sin multiplied to the point that God judged the entire earth. God offered salvation from the judgment aboard the Ark. All a person had to do was to recognize the position that his sins had put him in and humbly accept the open door of the Ark.

This account offers a parallel to our condition as humans today. God promised that He would never again judge the sin of mankind with a global flood. But another kind of judgment day is coming for all mankind.

Like Adam and Eve, each person on the earth has violated God's standard of righteousness—perfect obedience to His will. If you doubt your guilt before God, stop and think about the Ten Commandments as a summary of God's moral Law. Has God always been first in your life (Exodus 20:3–6)? Have you always obeyed and honored your parents (Exodus 20:12)? Have you ever stolen anything or told a lie (Exodus 20:15–16)? Jesus said that even if you look with lust you are guilty of committing adultery (Matthew 5:28). God judges not only our outward actions, but the intents of our heart. If we are honest, we will admit that we have broken His law uncountable times and we can never live up to His holy standard. Just as Paul said in Romans 3:23, "all have sinned and fall short of the glory of God."

God's punishment for the first sin involved both physical death and spiritual separation from God. Likewise, we die today as a penalty of sin. After we die physically, we will face God as our Judge, and He will judge our thoughts and words and deeds (Hebrews 9:27). This is the bad news; so now for the good news.

Just as God offered salvation from the judgment of the Flood by way of the single door of the Ark, He also offers salvation from the judgment to come through another "door." In John 10:9 Jesus referred to himself as "the door" and said, "If anyone enters by Me, he will be saved." So how does Jesus provide this offer of salvation?

After Adam and Eve had sinned, God killed animals and covered their shame with skins. This was the foreshadowing of the sacrificial system that was instituted through Moses to ceremonially cover over the sins of those who offered animal sacrifices in the Tabernacle and the Temple. But those sacrifices were just another picture of the ultimate sacrifice that God would provide to actually give people forgiveness of sin and a restored relationship with Him. He promised that Savior (Seed) to redeem the world way back in the Garden of Eden (Genesis 3:15) and then many times again by the Jewish prophets through the centuries.

Because the smallest sin is an infinitely offensive act against a perfectly holy God, the justice of God's judgment on sin can only be satisfied by a perfect sacrifice. That sacrifice came as God stepped into history in the person of Jesus Christ.

Jesus came to the earth, lived a perfectly holy life free of sin, and was then offered as the sacrificial "Lamb of God who takes away the sin of the world" (John 1:29). When Christ died on the Cross, the judgment for sin was poured out on Him. He drank the cup of wrath that was prepared for sinners like you and I. In his death, He is a substitute who bears our penalty. Since God's wrath is satisfied in Christ's perfect obedience and death, we no longer have to bear that penalty. This offer of salvation is extended to all men—but not all men will receive the gift (John 3:16–21). Death has now been defeated through the resurrection of Jesus Christ and eternal life is made available.

In order to receive the offer of forgiveness and eternal life, the good news of the gospel, God commands us to repent of our sins and place our faith in Christ. As Paul traveled on his missionary journeys he preached the need for "repentance toward God and faith toward our Lord Jesus Christ" (Acts 20:21). If you will humble yourself before God and place your faith in the life, death, and resurrection of Jesus Christ (1 Corinthians 15:3–4) you too will pass from death into life.

Just as God extended grace to Noah (Genesis 6:8), grace has also been extended to us in Christ's substitutionary death on the Cross. Salvation is a free gift that cannot be earned:

> For by grace you have been saved through faith, and that not of yourselves; it is the gift of God, not of works, lest anyone should boast (Ephesians 2:8–9).

Have you received that gift?